The Library of
NATIVE AMERICANS

The Wampanoag

of Massachusetts and Rhode Island

Janey Levy

The Rosen Publishing Group's
PowerKids Press™
New York

This book is dedicated to better understanding.

Special thanks to Tobias Vanderhoop of the Wampanoag Tribe of Aquinnah

Published in 2005 by The Rosen Publishing Group, Inc.
29 East 21st Street, New York, NY 10010

Photo and Illustration Credits: Cover, Peabody Museum, Harvard University Photo (T1672.1); p. 4, Mindy Liu; pp. 7, 17, 22, 43, 45, 53 Courtesy of Haffenreffer Museum of Anthropology, Brown University; pp. 9, 26, 31 Courtesy of Pilgrim Hall Museum, Plymouth, Massachusetts; p. 10 Natural History Museum, London, UK / Bridgeman Art Library; p. 13 © HIP / Scala / Art Resource, NY; pp. 14, 20, 25, 50 © AP/Wide World Photos; pp. 19, 34, 37, 41 © North Wind Picture Archives; p. 29 Private Collection / Ackermann and Johnson Ltd, London, UK / Bridgeman Art Library; p. 38 Hulton Archive / Getty Images; p. 47 Library of Congress Prints and Photographs Division; p. 48 National Anthropological Archives, Smithsonian Institution (03556400); pp. 54-55 © Richard Berenholtz/Corbis.

Book Design: Erica Clendening
Book Layout, Wampanoag Art, and Production: Mindy Liu
Contributing Editor: Kevin Somers

Library of Congress Cataloging-in-Publication Data

Levy, Janey.
   The Wampanoag of Massachusetts and Rhode Island / Janey Levy.
   p. cm. — (The library of Native Americans)
   Includes bibliographical references and index.
   Contents: An introduction to the Wampanoag people — Daily life — Encounters with Europeans — King Philip's War — The Wampanoag today.
   ISBN 1-4042-2871-3 (lib. bdg.)
   1. Wampanoag Indians—History—Juvenile literature. 2. Wampanoag Indians—Social life and customs—Juvenile literature. [1. Wampanoag Indians. 2. Indians of North America—New England.] I. Title. II. Series.

   E99.W2L48 2005
   974.4004'97348—dc22

            2003023893

Manufactured in the United States of America

Contents

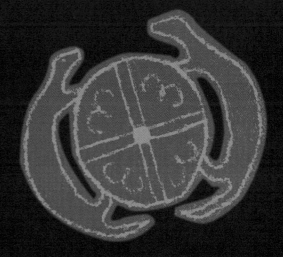

Where the Wampanoag Lived

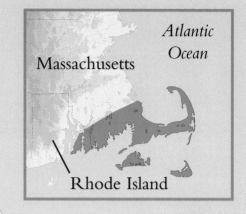

Massachusetts

Atlantic Ocean

Rhode Island

Wampanoag

Cape Cod Bay

Nantucket Sound

Martha's Vineyard

Nantucket Island

One

An Introduction to the Wampanoag

For thousands of years, the Wampanoag have occupied the region that is today eastern Rhode Island and southeastern Massachusetts, including Cape Cod, Martha's Vineyard, and Nantucket. At one time, there were more than 67 separate Wampanoag communities. They were known by the names of the places they inhabited, such as Aquinnah, Patuxet, Nantucket, Suconesset, and Mashpee.

In early written records, the Wampanoag were often referred to by the name Pokanoket, which means "place of the cleared land." This later changed to Wampanoo or Wampanoag, which means "people of the first light" or "people of the east."

Wampanoag communities were headed by *sachems*, who governed with the assistance of village councils. *Sachems* were responsible for the welfare of their people and could be leaders only as long as they had their people's support.

The family formed the heart of Wampanoag society. Extended families lived together, and work was divided among family members. Men and women each had their own tasks. Knowledge of these responsibilities and of Wampanoag traditions was handed down through the family from one generation to the next.

The lands where the Wampanoag lived were in areas of what are now known as Massachusetts and Rhode Island.

The Wampanoag

The arrival of European explorers and settlers in the 1500s changed Wampanoag life forever. Many early contacts between the Wampanoag and European traders and fishermen, who visited their coastal lands, were peaceful. Some European fishermen actually became members of Wampanoag communities. However, these kind of peaceful encounters with Europeans were not long lived. Inspired by the possibility of making large profits, captains of European trading ships began kidnapping Wampanoag people to sell as slaves in Europe. This soon became a common practice. Europeans began to establish permanent colonies on traditional Wampanoag lands in the early 1600s. The Wampanoag approached the situation according to their traditions—they observed the newcomers for several months to determine if they were friendly or not. In 1621, they signed a treaty with the Pilgrims. The Wampanoag shared their resources and their understanding of the land with their new neighbors. However, their generosity was not always repaid. The colonists used trickery and deception to take over more and more Wampanoag land. Diseases brought by the Europeans killed thousands of Wampanoag, sometimes destroying entire villages.

Today, only six Wampanoag communities survive in their peoples' ancient homeland. However, many Wampanoag live in cities and towns across the United States. Through the centuries of difficulty, the Wampanoag have remained independent and have preserved their cultural traditions. Special celebrations and events held in Wampanoag villages keep traditions alive for future generations and teach outsiders about the Wampanoag's rich heritage.

Origins of the People of the First Light

The first humans probably arrived in what is now New England between 10,000 and 12,000 years ago. Archaeologists call these early people Paleo-Indians. Paleo means ancient. The Paleo-Indians may have come to New England from the north or southwest areas. Several theories currently exist regarding these people's origins. However, there is not enough evidence at this time to say for sure which theory is correct.

At that time, the region was very cold. The earliest people were hunter-gatherers who moved from place to place as the seasons changed.

This stone figurine was found in southern New England. It is believed to be from a very early Wampanoag culture.

They made stone weapon points for hunting and stone tools for tasks like cleaning and scraping animal hides, sewing hides into clothes, and woodworking. In these early societies, men were the hunters. Women were responsible for tasks such as gathering wild plants and making clothes.

Archaeologists have uncovered cooking pits with burned bones, which tell us what kinds of animals the Paleo-Indians hunted. Bones of such huge animals as mastodon, as well as bones of caribou, musk ox, and giant beaver, have been found. Discoveries of clamshells and bones of waterbirds and shallow-water fish suggest that coastal Paleo-Indians were beginning to explore what foods the ocean offered.

Life in a Changing World

Between 10,000 and 3,000 years ago, life for the inhabitants of New England changed as the climate grew warmer. Huge animals like the mastodon could not survive in the warmer climate. Smaller animals became plentiful. The white-tailed deer emerged as the main food of the Indians. The ocean provided new kinds of fish and ocean mammals, like seals. The warmer climate also resulted in a greater variety of plants.

To make use of these new resources, the people began to make a wider variety of tools. The special tools they made were used for hunting, butchering, chopping wood, scraping hides, drilling shells, and building canoes. They even made special stone tools that were used for making other stone tools. Toward the end of this period, the Indians began to use stone tools to make pots out of a soft stone known as soapstone. The soapstone pots, as well as baskets and wooden bowls, were used to store food, although they could not be used for cooking. Women probably made the baskets, and men probably carved the wooden bowls and soapstone pots.

These stone objects, which date back more than 400 years, are some of the only surviving cultural examples of the Wampanoag and early native peoples.

The Wampanoag made use of a variety of food sources. Shellfish, among many other animals, were an important part of Wampanoag survival.

With more food and better tools, these latter-time Indians were able to form larger communities than had the Paleo-Indians. Archaeologists have found the remains of the small roundhouses they built. The size of the houses suggests that only a single family lived in each one.

The Early Wampanoag

Developments in technology led to many more changes in the lifestyle of New England Indians between about 3,000 years ago and 1,000 years ago. By the end of this period, a distinct Wampanoag culture had emerged.

During this era, Indians of the region began to fish using hooks and lines. They also began to hunt with bows and arrows. Bows and arrows proved to be better hunting tools than spears. They were more accurate and more powerful. The bow and arrow allowed hunters to attack their prey from a greater distance. The Indians also built dugout canoes, called *mishoons.* This advancement improved people's ability to harvest food from the waterways. The ocean and forests provided an increasingly varied diet. The ocean supplied foods such as sturgeon, striped bass, and shellfish. Animals such as gray seals, turtles, loons, and swans were also hunted in the seas. The forest provided animals such as deer, raccoons, red foxes, and gray squirrels.

Women began to use the region's abundant supply of clay to make pottery. The pottery was fired, or heated, to make it hard. To prevent the pottery from cracking as it was fired, women learned to add crushed shells or stones to the clay. Unlike the earlier baskets and bowls made of soapstone or wood, pottery could be used for cooking as well as for storage of food.

Women also began to plant and raise crops. The earliest crops grown were corn and beans. Later, squash and watermelons were added. The development of agriculture, along with the improved methods of hunting and fishing, meant that people did not have to move around as often in search of food. Raising crops allowed them to stay in one place until the crops were harvested. During the spring and summer, these early Wampanoag lived in fishing and farming villages along the coast. They then moved inland where they spent the fall and winter months. However, some communities may have established permanent villages where the people lived year round.

At the remains of villages from this era, archaeologists have uncovered tools made from stones not found in the region. Also discovered were objects made from copper, which came from the area around the Great Lakes. Objects made by the Wampanoag have also been found at great distances from Wampanoag lands. These finds tell us that the early Wampanoag were part of a vast trade network.

Early Wampanoag trade items included wampum, which were white or purple beads made from shells. The Wampanoag and many other early groups of people in North America valued wampum.

Purple beads were the most highly prized. The Wampanoag and other groups used the beads to make wampum belts, which recorded tribal history and were exchanged between leaders to honor special occasions.

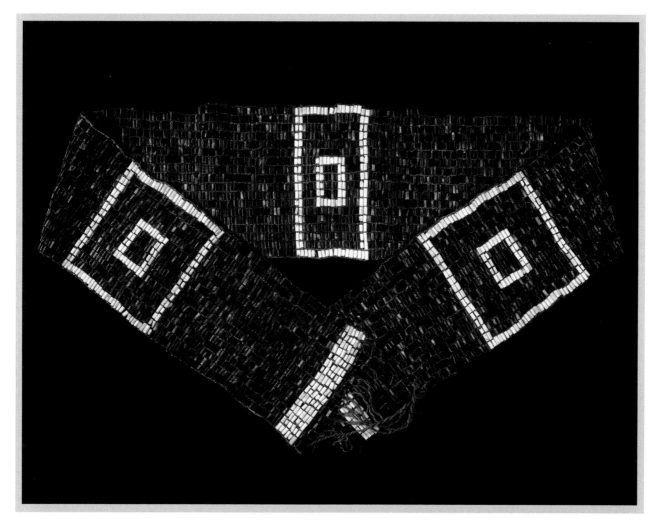

The highly-valued purple wampum were used to make belts such as this one. This belt was made sometime in the eighteenth century to celebrate a special event. The three rectangles suggest the joining together of three separate groups for war.

13

Two
Daily Life

The way of life that had emerged by about 1,000 years ago continued to provide a good life for the Wampanoag for many centuries. During the spring and summer months, people lived in farming villages on the coast, where they could take advantage of coastal fishing. They caught large fish such as cod, which can weigh more than 100 pounds and reach lengths of six feet or more. They also killed whales that had become stranded onshore.

In the fall, the village communities separated into extended family groups and moved to hunting territories farther inland. They spent the fall and winter in these territories, hunting and fishing in inland waterways. Each community lived, farmed, and hunted within a well-defined territory. The region was heavily populated by this time, and well-defined territories helped to reduce conflict.

There was no individual ownership of land in these territories. The community as a whole held the right to use the land, and it was used for the good of the entire community. However, each family was allowed the use of a particular area in which to raise crops.

This dugout canoe from the Plimoth Plantation living history museum in Massachusetts offers us a glimpse into the lives and culture of the Wampanoag who lived there more than 350 years ago.

The Creation of the Wampanoag Homeland

Wampanoag legend tells that a giant named Moshup created Martha's Vineyard and other nearby islands. There are different versions of the legend. According to one, Moshup was a just and wise man who excelled at feats of strength and bravery. People envious of Moshup believed his abilities to be magic. This led to conflict among some of his neighbors. Weary of the strife, Moshup, his wife, Squant, and their followers set out to find a new land, guided by the rising Sun. Finally, worn out by all the walking, Moshup stopped to look around him. As he did so, he dragged one of his feet, creating a channel that separated a section of land from the mainland. His footsteps created a chain of small islands. The largest, most beautiful island became the new home of Moshup, Squant, and their followers. Moshup named it Capawack, which means "refuge place." Capawack had forests, freshwater ponds, and sheltered fields for crops. Moshup captured whales swimming nearby for food and threw them against the Aquinnah Cliffs to kill them. The blood of the whales made the cliffs dark red. According to the legend, the bones of whales and other animals cooked by Squant and their children can still be found in the cliffs.

The Wampanoag record of their history is in the form of an oral tradition handed down from generation to generation through songs, dances, and spoken word. Legends often vary depending on who the storyteller is. The account of the creation legend cited above is a shortened version based on the legend provided by Helen Attaquin.

Moshup was the supernatural giant who carved out the Wampanoag homeland. In this illustration, Moshup wades out to a ship of Europeans who are threatening his homeland.

Hunting, Fishing, and Farming

Each family worked to provide its own food, clothing, and shelter. Those who were unable to work were cared for by family and friends. Men did the hunting and the fishing. Venison, or deer meat, was an important part of the Wampanoag diet. The men had different ways to hunt deer. One method was to make a trap with rope and cut down a nearby tree so that the deer would be drawn to the spot to eat the tree's leaves. The deer were captured when they stepped on the trap. Another method was for some of the men to chase the deer into a narrow path between hedges or rows of trees. Other men captured the deer when they became hemmed in by the hedges or trees.

Wampanoag men fished from their dugout canoes. They used spears to catch large fish. They also fished with bone hooks and lines made of plant fibers. In addition, Wampanoag men could catch many fish at a time using nets or a weir, a fenced enclosure.

Planting and raising crops were women's tasks, though sometimes men helped. This was particularly true of older men who were no longer able to hunt. Corn, beans, and squash—known as the Three Sisters—were traditionally planted together. The cornstalks acted as stakes for the bean vines. The squash vines covered the ground, helping to hold in moisture from rain and preventing erosion. The beans added nitrogen to the soil. Plants need nitrogen to grow. To protect the growing crops, women or older children stayed in small watch-houses in the fields to scare away the birds.

Wampanoag women and children also gathered shellfish and wild plants. Different wild foods were available at different times of the year. The availability of different foods offered the Wampanoag a varied diet. Spring and summer offered wild leeks and onions as well as many kinds of wild berries. These included strawberries, raspberries, huckleberries, and currants. Cranberries, acorns, and chestnuts were available in the fall. In late fall and winter, women and children dug up the roots of the Jerusalem artichoke. This is a type of sunflower whose roots were eaten as a vegetable.

Crop surpluses were preserved by drying. To dry corn, women pulled back the husk and braided

Here the Three Sisters—crops of corn, beans, and squash—are growing together in the traditional way that the Wampanoag women planted them.

20 In this re-creation of Wampanoag life in the seventeenth century, two modern-day Wampanoag women interpret the daily activities of sewing deerskin leggings and braiding hair.

it, so that the corn could be hung up to dry. Corn could also be spread on mats to dry. Dried corn, beans, and nuts were placed in large bags, which were then put in storage pits. The pits were dug in sandy hillsides so that rainwater would drain away from them. The pits were lined with old cattail mats. The Wampanoag placed more mats over the bags, then covered everything with soil.

The Wampanoag loved and indulged their children, yet they also taught them to be self-reliant. Fathers trained their sons to hunt, trap, fish, and make stone tools. Women taught their daughters to plant and raise crops, gather wild foods, cook, make clothing, and weave mats.

Housing

Families—which included parents, grandparents, children, and sometimes aunts and uncles—lived together in dome-shaped houses called *wetus.* A *wetu* had a frame made of cedar poles that were bent to form a curved or dome shape, then tied together with rope made from bark of the cedar tree. The outside of the frame was covered with sheets of bark or with mats made from cattails. The inside was covered with finely woven bulrush mats that were dyed. The double layer of mats helped to keep the *wetu* warm in winter and cool in summer. Building a *wetu* was men's work, although women wove the mats. *Wetus* were about 8 or 9 feet (2.4 or 2.7 meters) tall. Fires were built inside to provide warmth. Smoke escaped through an opening in the center of the roof. When it rained, a mat could be placed over the roof opening in such a way that it kept out the rain but still allowed the smoke to escape. *Wetus* were commonly about 12 feet (3.7 m) wide and 14 to 20 feet (4.3 to 6.1 m) long. Sometimes three or four families shared a single house. These *wetus* could be up to 100 feet (30.4 m) long and 30 feet (9.1 m) wide. Household goods varied widely. They included cooking and eating utensils such as clay pots, dishes, spoons, and ladles. Storage baskets, dried foods, and clothing, as well as toys and games, were also commonplace in the *wetus*.

This re-creation of a traditional *wetu* at the Haffenreffer Museum of Anthropology in Providence, Rhode Island, clearly shows how Wampanoag homes were framed and covered.

Household goods also included tools such as weapons, fishing gear, hide-working tools, and sewing kits. Sleeping platforms covered with animal hides and mats were the primary furniture items in these houses.

Travelers were warmly welcomed in Wampanoag homes. The Wampanoag belief in reciprocity meant that visitors were always invited to share whatever food the family had. People knew that one day they too might be travelers far from home who would need to rely on the kindness of strangers.

Government

Each Wampanoag community was led by a *sachem* chosen by the people from one of their leading families. Women as well as men could hold this position. *Sachems* were responsible for the welfare of everyone in the community. They settled disputes within their communities, assigned farming plots, and supervised planting and harvesting. *Sachems* also represented their people in all dealings with outsiders. *Sachems* who failed to show wise leadership lost the respect and support of their people.

Sachems were advised and assisted by councils who represented members of the community. Different groups, such as elders or women, would have separate councils. This ensured that every group had its say in decisions that affected the whole community. The communities were united in a confederacy under the leadership of a particularly well-respected *sachem*, who was known by the title of Massasoit, which meant "great leader." However, individual villages always had the right to withdraw from the confederacy.

The *sachem*'s life was not one of privilege. *Sachems* had to work for a living, just like everyone else. They received food and other goods through gifts, exchanges, and tributes. However, the Wampanoag idea of reciprocity did not allow them to keep this surplus to increase their personal wealth. Their status and respect from others depended on their sharing it with their community.

Religion

Reciprocity governed spiritual life as well. Wampanoag religious leaders, who were also healers, were called *powwaws*, which means "he or she is healing." They taught their people the importance of humility and thankfulness. For the Wampanoag, the people and the world around them were all part of the spiritual realm, not separate from it. The people were not above the other animals on Earth, but simply one tribe of beings among many. Hunters offered prayers for a successful hunt to the animal spirits. The animal spirits reciprocated by allowing themselves to be caught by the hunters. The people were taught to use natural resources with respect and care, so that there would be enough for future generations.

Every day was a day of thanksgiving for the Wampanoag. They gave thanks for the dawn, for the Sun and the Moon, for the rain that made plants grow, and for the crops when the people harvested them. They gave thanks for every animal they killed and honored its sacrifice.

The Wampanoag also celebrated many special days of thanksgiving throughout the year. Large numbers of people attended these celebrations, which included singing, dancing, and sharing food. The celebrations were also times for the people to reflect and to offer prayers of thanks to the Creator. The first special thanksgiving day of the year was the New Year, which the Wampanoag celebrated at the time of spring planting. There were many harvest celebrations, held after the work of the harvest had been completed. Strawberry Thanksgiving was held in early summer, when the first wild berries ripened. In midsummer, the Green Bean Harvest and Green Corn Harvest were celebrated. Cranberry Harvest was held in the fall, when the last wild berries ripened. The Wampanoag also had a special ceremony around the time of the winter solstice.

A traditional Wampanoag social dance is performed by modern Mashpee Wampanoag during a festival of thanksgiving.

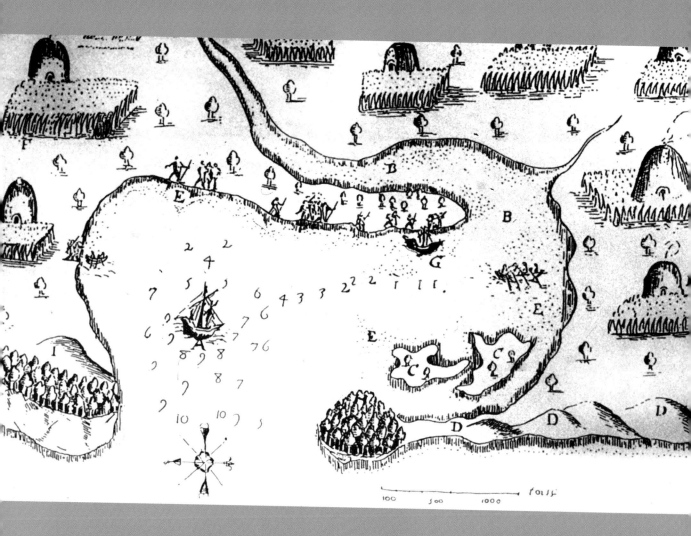

Three

Encounters with Europeans

The Wampanoag's first encounters with Europeans may have come as early as around A.D. 1000. The remains of a Viking settlement on the northern coast of Newfoundland, Canada, tell us that Viking explorers reached that part of North America's Atlantic coast. It is possible they journeyed far enough south to encounter the Wampanoag.

The Wampanoag may also have crossed paths with Italian explorer Giovanni da Verrazano, who sailed along the Atlantic coast in 1524. In his journal, Verrazano recorded meeting two native leaders on the coasts of present-day Rhode Island and Massachusetts—areas inhabited by the Wampanoag. Verrazano incorrectly called the leaders he met "kings." Europeans did not understand the native societies they encountered in North America and mistakenly applied European ideas to those societies.

Throughout the 1500s, European traders in search of furs and other items desired by wealthy Europeans journeyed to North America. European fishermen sometimes reached North America's eastern coast. The Wampanoag occasionally encountered some of these traders and fishermen. Relations with the fishermen were often without conflict. Relations with the traders, however,

In 1605, French explorer Samuel de Champlain drew a map for a place he called Port St. Louis. His map (left) shows Native American fields and houses located on the shores of what is now Cape Cod Bay. This place was later renamed Plymouth by the English.

presented problems. The Wampanoag greeted the strangers politely and tried to stay on good terms with them. However, the Europeans often committed crimes against the Wampanoag, including stealing and kidnapping.

The Early 1600s

In 1602, an English ship commanded by Bartholomew Gosnold explored Cape Cod and the nearby islands, including Martha's Vineyard and the Elizabeth Islands. John Brereton, a member of Gosnold's crew, described the generosity of the Wampanoag in his journal. In keeping with their traditions, the Wampanoag shared their food with the members of Gosnold's crew who went ashore. They also gave the visitors gifts, such as tobacco pipes and deerskins. The Englishmen did not behave as well, however. They repaid the Wampanoag's generosity by stealing a canoe.

Three years after the encounter with Gosnold and his crew, French explorer Samuel de Champlain arrived. The book Champlain later wrote about his journey described the Wampanoag houses and cornfields he saw at Patuxet. Unfortunately, the Europeans once again stole from the Wampanoag.

In 1611, the Wampanoag were again visited by English explorers and traders. A ship commanded by Edward Harlow landed on Martha's Vineyard. Harlow's crew kidnapped several Wampanoag men, including a *sachem* named Epenow, and took them back to

London. Epenow did not want to remain in England. He made a plan to get the English to take him back to Martha's Vineyard. From there,

he would be able to escape. Epenow knew of the Englishmen's hunger for gold, so he told them that there was much gold to be had on Martha's Vineyard. In 1614, an English ship returned to Martha's Vineyard to hunt for the gold, bringing Epenow along as a guide. While the ship was at anchor off the coast of the island, Epenow escaped and returned to his people.

More kidnappings of Wampanoag occurred in 1614. An expedition led by English explorer John Smith reached New England to map the coast, trade for furs, and begin fishing operations. After Smith returned

Lemuel-Francis Abbott painted this portrait of English explorer John Smith in the late eighteenth century.

to England, men he left behind in New England kidnapped 27 Wampanoag men to sell as slaves in Spain. Among the captives was a Patuxet man named Tisquantum, called Squanto by the English. Tisquantum managed to escape from his captors, fleeing to England. He spent five years there before returning to his homeland in the summer of 1619 as a guide for an English trader named Thomas Dermer.

When Tisquantum returned to his native village of Patuxet, which was once home to 2,000 people, he found it abandoned. In 1616, an epidemic of an unknown disease brought by Europeans had erupted in southern Maine. Over the next two years, it spread through the middle of Wampanoag territory. Patuxet and many other Wampanoag communities were completely destroyed. Communities that survived suffered terrible losses.

The enormous losses in their population brought other dangers to the Wampanoag. They feared that their traditional enemies, the Narraganset, would take advantage of the situation to launch a war aimed at conquering them. The arrival of more English traders and colonists was an additional cause for concern.

The Pilgrims Come

In the summer of 1620, Thomas Dermer and Tisquantum traveled through New England and returned to Martha's Vineyard. An Abenaki *sachem* named Samoset traveled with them. Epenow recognized

Dermer because Dermer worked for the man who had kept Epenow as a prisoner in England. Fearing that Dermer had come to capture him again, Epenow led an attack on the Englishmen. Dermer was wounded, several of his men were killed, and Tisquantum and Samoset were captured. Epenow sent Tisquantum and Samoset to Ousamequin, who was the Massasoit, or great leader.

A few months later, the Wampanoag observed the arrival of another English ship. This was the *Mayflower*, bringing the Pilgrims. The strangers came ashore at Patuxet, where they began to cut down trees and build houses. The Pilgrims named their settlement Plymouth.

This painting by an unknown artist, *The Landing of the Pilgrims*, was made in 1820 for a celebration of the two-hundredth anniversary of the landing of the Pilgrims.

The Wampanoag

Though strangers had come many times before, they did not usually build houses. These strangers were also unusual in that their families were with them. Wampanoag men would never take women and children to a place where they would be in danger. Therefore, they hoped the presence of the strangers' families meant that the strangers did not plan to commit acts of violence. Still, the Wampanoag thought it wise to keep an eye on the strangers. Councils met to discuss the events, and men were sent to watch the strangers and report what they saw to the councils.

By the spring of 1621, the Wampanoag had come to a decision—they would actively seek an alliance with the Pilgrims. The Wampanoag population had been so reduced by the epidemic of 1618 that they felt constantly threatened by the Narraganset. The Wampanoag believed the Pilgrims—with their powerful weapons—would be a helpful ally against an attack by the Narraganset. Samoset, who could speak English, was sent to speak with the Pilgrims. The Pilgrims, also fearful of the Narraganset, welcomed the proposal and agreed to meet with the Wampanoag, including Ousamequin, his brother Quadequina, and Tisquantum.

At the meeting, the Pilgrims presented gifts to Ousamequin, whom they called by his title, Massasoit. As a result of this, many of them incorrectly believed that Ousamequin's name was Massasoit. Both sides agreed to a treaty in which each group promised to treat the other group honorably, to leave weapons behind when they visited each other, and to help each other if they were attacked.

The Treaty of 1621

This account of the 1621 treaty between the Wampanoag and the Pilgrims was recorded by Pilgrim leader William Bradford.

1. That neither he [Ousamequin] nor any of his should injure or do hurt to any of our people [Pilgrims].
2. And if any of his did hurt to any of ours, he should send the offender, that we might punish him.
3. That if any of our tools were taken away when our people were at work, he should cause them to be restored; and if ours did any harm to any of his, we would do the like to them.
4. If any did unjustly war against him, we would aid him; if any did war against us, he should aid us.
5. He should send to his neighbor confederates, to certify them of this, that they might not wrong us, but might be likewise comprised in the conditions of peace.
6. That when their men came to us, they should leave their bows and arrows behind them, as we should do our pieces when we came to them.

Lastly, that doing thus, King James would esteem of him as his friend and ally.

The Wampanoag

A period of cooperation and cultural influences followed the treaty. The Pilgrims actively worked to convert the Wampanoag to Christianity. The Pilgrims successfully changed the traditional way of life for many Wampanoag people. These converted Wampanoag were called "praying Indians" by the colonists. They were encouraged by the Pilgrims to wear English clothes, live in houses like those built by the English, and obey English laws and land-ownership practices. By accepting these things, the "praying Indians" were no longer living according to Wampanoag traditions. Yet they were not fully a part of English society either.

34 This hand-colored woodcut shows the Wampanoag and Plymouth Colony leaders at the signing of the Treaty of 1621. Sharing was a traditional part of agreements in the Wampanoag culture. Notice that Ousamequin is offering his pipe to the colonial leader.

Squanto's Fate

Tisquantum, called Squanto by the English, stayed with the colonists. He acted as their interpreter and taught them what they needed to know to survive in the new land. Most of the Pilgrims were craftspeople, not farmers or hunters. Tisquantum taught them when and how to plant and fertilize crops. He also taught them where to find the best fish and how to catch them in traps. This newfound standing with the colonists put Tisquantum in a position of great power. Unfortunately, Tisquantum tried to take advantage of this power to increase his personal wealth. Tisquantum used his people's fear for his own gain. He would promise to put in a good word to the colonists on a Wampanoag's behalf in exchange for payment. He also told the Wampanoag that the colonists had a terrible disease in their storehouse and that he was the only one who could stop the colonists from using it. At the same time, he told the Pilgrims that Ousamequin and the Narraganset were plotting against them. Hobbamock, a Wampanoag warrior and councilor who lived near the Pilgrims, told them that this could not be true. Tisquantum tried to prove that Massasoit was planning to attack by staging a hoax. He had one of his friends come running out of the woods covered with blood, claiming that Massasoit was attacking. When Tisquantum's lies were revealed, an angry Ousamequin demanded that the Pilgrims return Tisquantum to the Wampanoag for punishment, in keeping with the treaty. The Pilgrims, who depended heavily on Tisquantum's services, were not eager to give him up. The matter still had not been settled when Tisquantum died in the autumn of 1622.

The Wampanoag

Cooperation between the groups did not last and cultural differences turned into conflict. Many colonists came to live and build communities on Wampanoag land. Problems arose as colonists allowed their livestock to run loose and destroy Wampanoag crops. The Wampanoag wanted the colonists to build fences to contain their cattle. The Pilgrims said it was the Wampanoag's job to build the fences to keep the livestock out of their crops.

In spite of the many offenses committed by the colonists, Ousamequin honored the treaty because he was a man of his word. He also believed it was best for his people to avoid war if it was at all possible. Ousamequin died in 1661, having honored the treaty for 40 years.

After Ousamequin's death, his eldest son, Wamsutta, became *sachem*. Wamsutta, also known by the English name Alexander, did not hold this position for long. In 1662, a group of Pilgrims came to "invite" Wamsutta to meet with leaders in Plymouth. Wamsutta and several other Wampanoag were forced at gunpoint to travel to Plymouth with the Pilgrims. On the trip, Wamsutta became ill. He died on his journey home. The Wampanoag, saddened and angry, believed that Wamsutta had been poisoned by the English. Wamsutta's brother Metacomet, also known by the English name Philip, became *sachem*. Like his father, Metacomet believed that keeping the peace was the best thing for his people. He worked hard to avoid war. However, the problems between the Wampanoag and the colonists finally became so great that it was no longer possible to avoid war. The war became known to the English as King Philip's War.

Illustrations, such as this woodcut, often wrongly represent the culture of the Wampanoag people. Here, Ousamequin is dressed more like a Native American of the western plains than a traditional Wampanoag.

Four

King Philip's War

By 1662, when Metacomet became *sachem*, relations between the Wampanoag and the colonists at Plymouth had soured. The steady expansion of the colony was consuming more and more Wampanoag land. Colonists occupied traditional Wampanoag fall and winter hunting territories and even took over farmland that the Wampanoag had cleared for their crops. The colonists claimed that they had acquired the land legally and had signed land deeds to prove it. In these land deals, however, the colonists often took advantage of the fact that the Wampanoag could not read English. They obtained more land than the Wampanoag realized by lying to the Wampanoag about how much land was covered by the deeds.

Debt also led *sachems* to sell off Wampanoag land. The economy of the region had changed. The fur trade, which had benefited both the Wampanoag and the Pilgrims, was no longer an important part of the economy. The Massachusetts colonists now focused on trade with Europe. Many Wampanoag went to work for colonists. They were paid with alcohol, which got them drunk and left them with no way to pay for European goods. Growing debt forced many Wampanoag into indentured servitude and caused leaders like Wamsutta and Metacomet to sell tribal lands to pay their debts.

This portrait of *sachem* Metacomet, called King Philip by the English, was illustrated around 1670, a time when he was still struggling to keep the peace. **39**

The Wampanoag tried to use peaceful means to fight this immoral taking of their lands. They had grown to understand the colonists' court system and believed that the colonists would have to honor Wampanoag land claims that were upheld by the colonists' own legal system. Beginning in the late 1650s, Plymouth court records show many cases brought by the Wampanoag against the colonists. Disagreements concerned property boundaries, cattle allowed by colonists to roam freely on Wampanoag lands, and illegal purchases of Wampanoag lands by colonists.

Unfortunately, the Wampanoag's legal efforts did not succeed in stopping the English from taking the tribe's land. Relations between the Wampanoag and the colonists worsened as problems increased during the 1660s and 1670s. In spite of all this, Metacomet struggled to maintain the treaty made between his father and the Pilgrims, because he still believed peace was in the best interests of his people. Finally, Metacomet realized that only the use of force would stop the English from taking everything. He began to build an alliance of tribes to wage war against the colonists.

First Sparks of War

In January 1675, events occurred that made tensions boil between the Wampanoag and the colonists. A Christianized Wampanoag named John Sassamon was found dead in a frozen pond at Assawompset (now Middleboro, Massachusetts). Many historians believe that Sassamon had, at one time, been one of Metacomet's councilors. Whether he had or not, he wasn't at the time of his death.

The English considered Sassamon to be one of them since he was a Christian. Moreover, the murder had taken place on land controlled by the colonists. They believed this gave them the right to punish his killers under the terms of the 1621 treaty. The English arrested three Wampanoag men who they believed were the killers. These three men were tried, found guilty, and, on June 8, 1675, were executed. Mattashunannamo, Tobias, and Wampapaquan were tried at the court at Plymouth. The trial was conducted in a hasty manner. It relied heavily on questionable evidence and was tried by a jury whose lawfulness was suspect.

The Native Americans who clashed with the English during King Philip's war were not prepared for the fierce way the English fought. This hand-colored engraving shows a violent representation of a conflict between the two groups.

Metacomet and the other Wampanoag were furious. Even though Sassamon was a Christian, and perhaps a spy for the English, he was still a Wampanoag. This meant the Wampanoag had the right, under the 1621 treaty, to punish whoever killed him.

Rumors that the English planned to arrest Metacomet for arranging the murder of Sassamon followed the trial. Then in June 1675, a colonist near the English settlement at Swansea shot and killed a Wampanoag. With this, the Wampanoag and their allies finally went to war with the colonists.

War

Metacomet's warriors first attacked Swansea, Massachusetts. They went on to raid other colonial villages, usually settlements along the edge of English territory. In response, the English mounted an attack on Metacomet's home village at Mount Hope. Along the way, the English soldiers burned other Wampanoag villages. On the mainland, colonists also rounded up "praying Indians," whom they did not trust to remain loyal to the English side, and forced them to live on "plantations of confinement" set up on islands in Boston Harbor and Plymouth Harbor.

The Wampanoag were horrified by the savagery of the English way of fighting. The Wampanoag conducted war on a limited scale. They killed few of their male enemies, and women and children were spared. In contrast, the colonists burned native villages and killed hundreds of women and children in addition to the men. They also burned the Wampanoag's fields of corn.

In December 1675, a terrible battle occurred. The colonists attacked a Narraganset fort, even though the Narraganset had signed a peace treaty with the colonists earlier that year and had not joined Metacomet's war. However, the Narraganset were allowing Wampanoag women and children to stay in their fort. The English believed this made the Narraganset their enemy. The colonists demanded that the Narraganset turn over the Wampanoag women

In 1896, George W. Bardwell made this illustration of the Battle of Bloody Brook fought during King Philip's war. The illustration appeared in Alma Holman Burton's *Massasoit, a Romantic Story of the Indians of New England.*

and children. When the Narraganset refused, the colonists attacked. The battle became known as the Great Swamp Fight or Great Swamp Massacre. More than 600 Narraganset warriors and at least 20 *sachems* were killed in the battle. The colonists also suffered heavy losses and were not able to pursue those Narraganset who managed to escape from the fort. Many of these survivors, including the *sachem* Canonchet, joined Metacomet's warriors in the fight against the colonists.

The winter of 1675–1676 was a horrible one for the Wampanoag. Many people were starving because the colonists had destroyed their crops. Because their fields were still occupied by the English in the spring, the Wampanoag could not plant new crops. Canonchet volunteered to sneak back to Rhode Island where his people had corn hidden and bring that corn to Metacomet's people. However, he was captured by the English and killed.

Many Wampanoag became discouraged. Weary and weakened by hunger, some Wampanoag surrendered to the colonists. Many of these, along with others who had been captured by the colonists, were killed. Others were sold as slaves to work on sugar plantations in the West Indies.

Fighting continued through the spring and summer of 1676. In August 1676, the English finally caught Metacomet. He was killed and his head was cut off. His head was mounted on a pole and displayed at Plymouth for 25 years, as a warning to others who would try to stop the spread of English settlement.

This illustration showing King Philip's death was printed in *New England Magazine* in July 1898. The artist is Howard Pyle, famous for illustrating *The Merry Adventures of Robin Hood* and *King Arthur and His Knights*.

King Philip's War ended with Metacomet's death, but the fighting continued for two more years. Colonists hunted down Metacomet's allies and killed them. English soldiers attacked the Nashua during peace talks in 1676, killing 200 of them and selling the prisoners as slaves. Other English soldiers attacked the Pennacook, who had not taken sides in the war. The fighting was finally ended by the Peace of Casco, which was signed on April 12, 1678. The Wampanoag's brave effort to protect their homeland had failed.

Life After the War

King Philip's War nearly destroyed the Wampanoag people. In 1600, there had been around 20,000 Wampanoag. Only a few hundred survived the war. After the English victory, the colonists regarded all Native Americans as either enemies or conquered subjects. Captured Wampanoag were shipped to the West Indies as slaves or forced to become indentured servants on colonists' farms. The remaining Wampanoag on the mainland were forced onto plantations. If they went beyond the reservation's boundaries, they were forced to give three months' service to whoever caught them. Only the Wampanoag who had not taken sides during the war, including those on Martha's Vineyard and Nantucket, were allowed to remain where they were.

After the war, many Wampanoag became Christians. Some did this because they wanted to. Others did so because it allowed them to keep their communities whole, since villages of "praying Indians" were permitted to stay together. They adapted Christianity to fit Wampanoag community structures and values, so that they could preserve as much of their traditional culture as possible.

For the Wampanoag people forced onto plantations, life was often very difficult. Non-Indian officials were put in charge of the plantations. They managed the Wampanoag's land and money, and represented the Wampanoag in all dealings with outsiders. Not surprisingly, this system often failed the Wampanoag. On some plantations, they suffered terrible poverty. In other communities, diseases brought by colonists caused many deaths. An epidemic of an unknown disease destroyed the community on Nantucket in 1763.

Colonists continued to deal dishonestly with the Wampanoag. Wampanoag sometimes leased their land to colonists for farming or logging. Colonists did not always pay what they had agreed to pay, and sometimes colonists simply refused to leave the land after the lease ended.

Wampanoag Survival

In spite of these hardships, the Wampanoag found ways to keep their culture alive.

This statue of Ousamequin called *Statue to Massasoit*, stands in Plymouth, Massachusetts. This Wampanoag leader who struggled to avoid conflict symbolizes the strength of the Wampanoag people.

Some communities vanished, but others grew, including Mashpee on Cape Cod and Aquinnah (Gay Head) at the western tip of Martha's Vineyard. Mashpee was constantly at odds with the colonists. Then, around 1746, colonial authorities took over running the community, as they did with many other Wampanoag communities. This led to the usual land disagreements between the Wampanoag and colonists. The Mashpee Wampanoag took the colonists to court many times. Sometimes they won their cases. Sometimes they did not. In 1833, the Woodlot Riot occurred. For years, colonists had been illegally taking wood from Wampanoag lands. In 1833, the Mashpee Wampanoag caught a group of colonists with a wagon full of wood, unloaded the

48 Ousamequin's descendant Tiliwima wears traditional clothing and feather headdress in this 1885 photograph.

wood, and sent the colonists away empty-handed. In 1867, the Mashpee Wampanoag formed the Mashpee Manufacturing Company, which made baskets, brooms, woodenwares, and other items.

In 1870, the Massachusetts General Court took the land occupied by the Aquinnah Wampanoag and created the town of Gay Head. The court also took the land occupied by the Mashpee Wampanoag and created the town of Mashpee. The Aquinnah and Mashpee Wampanoag objected, because actions such as this were forbidden by a U.S. law passed in 1790, but the change took place anyway. Since the Wampanoag formed the majority of the population in both towns, they were able to maintain political control of their communities.

Throughout the 1900s, the Wampanoag took steps to keep their culture alive. They continued many Wampanoag customs through their crafts and their farming. In the 1950s and 1960s, the Mashpee Wampanoag held classes to teach traditional ways to their children. These classes had a great impact on the Wampanoag children. The children grew up with a strengthened sense of identity. This made for stronger, more outspoken leadership in the communities.

In 1972, the Wampanoag Tribal Council of Gay Head was formed to encourage Wampanoag self-government, to make sure that Wampanoag culture and history are preserved, to gain official recognition of the tribe from the U.S. government, and to get tribal lands returned to the Wampanoag.

Five

The Wampanoag Today

Today, there are about 4,000 Wampanoag people. Some live in the traditional Wampanoag homelands. Others have been forced to leave because there are few jobs available in their homelands and the cost of living is often high. The Wampanoag who remain in their traditional homelands are taking many steps to strengthen their communities and improve life for their people. For example, the Education Department of the Wampanoag Tribe of Gay Head (Aquinnah) helps tribal members find training and employment opportunities. The Aquinnah Cultural Center hopes to create more jobs for tribal members by developing tourism. In 1987, the Aquinnah Wampanoag succeeded in gaining federal recognition as a tribe. This means that they can seek compensation from the federal government for lands that were taken from them illegally. In 1998, the Aquinnah Wampanoag also got the Massachusetts government to recognize their heritage by agreeing to officially change the name of Gay Head back to its Wampanoag name, Aquinnah.

A tribal council governs the Wampanoag tribe. The chairperson, vice chairperson, secretary, treasurer, and seven members are elected by the people. The council also includes the Chief and

Native American Chuck Jones dances during a fundraising powwow for the Watuppa Wampanoag Reservation in Freetown, Massachusetts.

Medicine Man, who hold their positions for life. Council meetings are open to all members of the tribe, so that everyone can have a say in the decisions. General meetings of all tribal members are also held, as are public hearings on special issues. Tribal members also vote on issues that need the approval of the entire tribe.

Family, religion, and traditional arts continue to play important roles in Wampanoag life. Powwows and celebrations such as the Legends of Moshup Pageant, Strawberry Thanksgiving, and Cranberry Day are held throughout the year. A number of Wampanoag also perform ceremonies that reflect the old traditions of their ancestors. Unlike the public celebrations, which outsiders may attend, these sacred ceremonies are for Wampanoag only. In addition to these celebrations and ceremonies, many Wampanoag continue to practice traditional arts such as basketry, pottery, and beadwork. Traditional arts have also been expanded to include new forms, such as pottery jewelry.

The modern Wampanoag work in many ways to maintain and teach their history and traditions. For example, the Aquinnah Wampanoag have developed a Cultural Resource Protection Program. This program will carry out the tribe's responsibilities under federal law for maintaining and protecting tribal cultural resources. The Aquinnah Wampanoag also have a Tribal Historic Preservation Officer. The officer's duties include creating a list of all historical and culturally significant properties on tribal lands; nominating Wampanoag properties to be included on the National Register of Historic Places; and providing public information, education, and training in historic preservation.

The Aquinnah Wampanoag have also set up the Aquinnah Cultural Center. The center offers classes and activities for tribal members as a way to renew and strengthen cultural traditions. Exhibits, public programs, and a library are also planned for the center.

Some Wampanoag also work to teach the public about Wampanoag history and traditions by taking part in the programs offered at the Plimoth Plantation living history museum. The museum includes a re-creation of a Pilgrim village as it would have

Brown University student Nitana Hicks of the Mashpee Wampanoag stands before a drumming group at a powwow.

53

The Wampanoag

been in 1627, along with Hobbamock's Homesite, a re-creation of a Wampanoag homesite of the 1620s. Hobbamock's Homesite actually sits on a spot where ancestors of the Wampanoag lived 8,000 years ago. Here, modern Wampanoag men and women teach visitors about Wampanoag culture through conversation, craft activities, and storytelling.

Through these many different practices, the modern Wampanoag maintain their traditions, strengthen their communities, and help to teach outsiders about their rich heritage. They want to keep their culture alive and strong, so that future generations can take pride in who they are.

A variety of beautiful northeastern coastal areas, such as Aquinnah in Martha's Vineyard, Massachusetts, are still home to Wampanoag people today.

Timeline

12,000 to 10,000 years ago	The first people arrive in New England.
Around 3,000 to 1,000 years ago	Indians of New England begin to use bows and arrows, make pottery, and raise crops. A distinct Wampanoag culture emerges.
A.D. 1000	Vikings reach Newfoundland, Canada. They may have traveled far enough south to encounter Wampanoag.
1524	Italian explorer Giovanni da Verrazano travels along coasts of Rhode Island and Massachusetts. He records encounters with people who may be Wampanoag.
1602	Crew of English ship commanded by Bartholomew Gosnold encounters Wampanoag on Cape Cod and Martha's Vineyard. Wampanoag feed Englishmen and give them gifts. Englishmen steal Wampanoag canoe.

Samuel de Champlain explores Cape Cod.

Epenow and other Wampanoag men kidnapped by crew of English ship commanded by Edward Harlow.

Epenow tricks English into taking him back to Martha's Vineyard, where he escapes. Other Englishmen kidnap 27 Wampanoag men to sell as slaves in Spain. One, Tisquantum, manages to escape to England.

Epidemic of disease brought by Europeans kills thousands of Wampanoag and destroys entire villages.

Tisquantum and Samoset captured by Epenow after battle with their English captors. Pilgrims arrive.

Wampanoag and Pilgrims agree to treaty.

Wampanoag grand *sachem* Ousamequin dies. His son Wamsutta becomes grand *sachem*.

Wamsutta dies. His brother Metacomet becomes grand *sachem*.

The Wampanoag

1675–1676	Metacomet leads an alliance of New England tribes in war to end English settlement and seizure of native lands.
1678	Peace of Casco brings final end to fighting in New England.
1746	Colonial authorities take over Mashpee Wampanoag.
1833	The Mashpee Wampanoag stage the Woodland Riot.
1870	Massachusetts General Court takes lands of Aquinnah Wampanoag and creates town of Gay Head. Court also takes over lands of Mashpee Wampanoag and creates town of Mashpee.
1972	Wampanoag Tribal Council of Gay Head organized.
1987	Aquinnah Wampanoag succeed in obtaining federal recognition as tribe.
1998	Aquinnah Wampanoag force Massachusetts to change name of Gay Head back to its original Wampanoag name, Aquinnah.

Glossary

alliance (uh-LY-uhns) An agreement between two or more groups in order to achieve a common goal.

archaeologists (ar-kee-AH-luh-jihsts) People who study the buildings and objects left by people who lived long ago in order to learn about their culture.

confederacy (kuhn-FEH-duh-ruh-see) A group of people or nations that have agreed to unite.

confinement (kuhn-FINE-ment) A place where someone or something is kept within certain bounds.

councils (KOWN-sulz) Groups of people who gather to discuss laws and make government decisions.

epidemic (eh-puh-DEH-mihk) A quick spreading of a disease to many people in a population.

erosion (ih-ROH-zhuhn) The loss of soil caused by wind or water.

evidence (EH-vuh-duhns) Proof of what happened.

expedition (ek-spuh-DISH-uhn) A long journey for a special purpose, such as exploring.

fired (FY-ird) Baked something such as clay at very high temperatures, until it is hard and dry.

generations (jeh-nuh-RAY-shuhnz) Groups of people born around the same time. Children are one generation, their parents are another, and their grandparents are still another.

indentured servant (in-DENT-shuhrd SIR-vuhnt) Someone who must work for someone else in order to pay off a debt.

lease (LEES) A legal contract that says someone can use land belonging to someone else for a certain period of time. The contract also states that the person using the land must pay the person who owns the land.

nation (NAY-shuhn) A group of people who share the same beliefs and who follow the same laws.

plantation of confinement (plan-TAY-shuhn UV kuhn-FYN-muhnt) An area of land set aside to keep a group of people as prisoners.

point (POYNT) An arrowhead or spearhead.

reciprocity (reh-suh-PRAH-suh-tee) The belief that everything received or taken requires something offered or given in exchange.

reservation (reh-zuhr-VAY-shuhn) A piece of land set aside by the government on which Native Americans are forced to live.

sachems (SAY-chuhmz) A leader of a Native American tribe.

solstice (SOHL-stuhs) Either of two days during the year when the difference between the number of hours of daylight and the number of hours of darkness is greatest.

weir (WEHR) A fence or enclosure set in a waterway to capture fish.

Resources

BOOKS

Bourne, Russell. *The Red King's Rebellion: Racial Politics in New England 1675–1678.* New York: Oxford University Press, 1991.

Mills, Earl, et al. *Son of Mashpee: Reflections of Chief Flying Eagle, a Wampanoag.* North Falmouth, MA: Word Studio, 1996.

Weinstein-Farson, Laurie. *The Wampanoag.* New York: Chelsea House Publishers, 1988.

Ziner, Feenie. *Squanto.* North Haven, CT: Linnet Books, 1988.

ORGANIZATIONS

Wampanoag Tribe of Gay Head (Aquinnah)
20 Black Brook Road
Aquinnah, MA 02535-1546
(508) 645-9265

Plimoth Plantation
PO Box 1620
Plymouth, MA 02362
(508) 746-1622

WEB SITES

Due to the changing nature of Internet links, PowerKids Press
has developed an online list of Web sites related to the subject of this
book. This site is updated regularly. Please use this link to access the
list:

www.powerkidslinks.com/lna/wampanoag

Index